Science in Colonial America

Brendan January

PACIFIC
OCEAN

Louisiana Purchase

The United States
in 1783

Thirteen Colonies

ATLANTIC
OCEAN

Spanish Florida

N

0   200 km
0   200 mi

Science in Colonial America

Brendan January

Science of the Past

FRANKLIN WATTS

A Division of Grolier Publishing
New York • London • Hong Kong • Sydney
Danbury, Connecticut

Visit Franklin Watts on the Internet at: http://publishing.grolier.com

Maps created by XNR Productions Inc.

Library of Congress Cataloging-in-Publication Data

January, Brendan, 1972–
       Science in Colonial America /Brendan January
          p. cm. — (Science of the past)
       Includes bibliographical references and index.
       Summary: Describes the scientific contributions made by people in colonial America, including medicine, astronomy, natural history, and electricity.
       ISBN 0-531-11525-9 (lib. bdg.)   0-531-15940-X (pbk.)
       1. Science—United States—History—Eighteenth century—Juvenile literature.
2. Scientists—United States—Biography—Juvenile literature. [1. Science—History.
2. Scientists.]   I. Title. II. Series.
Q127.U6J35   1999
509.73'09'033—dc21

                                         97-44047
                                            CIP
                                            AC

CONTENTS

chapter 1

European Science Comes to North America

The *Mayflower* landed along the coast of what is now Massachusetts.

Almost 400 years ago, wooden ships packed with European settlers arrived off the coast of North America. At first, life was extremely difficult. The long voyage left many passengers sick and weak, and the colonists struggled to build homes and find food. In Massachusetts, the Pilgrims received help from the local Indian tribes. In Jamestown, Virginia, however, the Indians thought of the settlers as invaders. Few Jamestown colonists dared venture outside the protective walls of the town. As a result, the settlers had trouble surviving. Of the 10,000 people who traveled to early Jamestown, fewer than 2,000 were alive 20 years later.

Within a few decades, however, living conditions

A Native American greets the Pilgrims.

In the 1660s, Boston was a busy trading center.

had improved. Boatloads of new *colonists* arrived, bringing fresh supplies and tools. With axes, saws, and guns, they began clearing forests and planting crops. New towns sprang up, and the European population spread. Port cities, such as Boston, New York, Philadelphia, and Charleston, grew into busy centers of trade. Slowly, thirteen colonies developed along the eastern coast of North America.

Sir Francis Bacon and the Age of Reason

At that time, science in Europe was heavily influenced by an English *philosopher* named Sir Francis Bacon. Bacon wrote that people should study the world closely. They should carefully watch how flowers bloom, clouds form, and planets move. Through observation, *natural philosophers*—people we would call scientists today—could determine the laws of nature. He believed that this knowledge could be used to improve people's lives.

Bacon urged people to use reason—a logical thought process—as they observed the world around them. He believed that superstition, emotion, and unreasonable fears interfere with accurate observation. Bacon's ideas became well known throughout Europe.

Sir Francis Bacon was a respected British philosopher and writer. He lived from 1561 to 1626.

Soon, people were making observations and scribbling them down in notebooks. Excitedly, they wrote letters to interested friends, sharing their results. Some of them began gathering in places where they could exchange their views and learn from each other. In 1660 the Royal Society, a scientific organization, was founded in London. Soon, groups dedicated to science sprang up all over Europe. A new scientific age was dawning.

The American colonists worked hard to build communities like New York City.

Science in Colonial America

During this period in the American colonies, few people gave serious attention to science. Colonial Americans were too busy establishing communities and doing the hard work necessary for survival. They had no time to erect libraries and universities, and little money to spend on scientific study. One colonial American wrote to an Englishman: "We want hands, my lord, more than heads."

Colonial settlers had no desire to work on complicated scientific theories that no one else would understand. The science that developed in colonial America was very practical. The people thought of science as a tool, as a way to make their lives easier. Sailors, traders, and trappers needed knowledge of *astronomy* and math to cross dense forests and navigate rivers and oceans. Other settlers studied North American plants with the hope of discovering medical remedies. These colonists used science to solve the problems they faced every day.

Colonial American science was also *democratic.* The colonists wanted a society that offered everyone equal opportunities. Anyone could participate in local government. Since most colonists could read, they paid careful attention to newspaper articles that presented both sides of debates on important issues.

This same democratic attitude applied to the study of science. In the colonies, science was not dominated by a small group of thinkers. Colonial newspapers often printed articles that discussed scientific ideas. Lecturers traveled all over the colonies, performing experiments that stunned audiences. In colonial America, anyone could study science. It required only curiosity and hard work.

The colonial American view of science encouraged people to ask questions about the world around them. The science and scientific attitude that developed in the American colonies laid the groundwork for some of the most revolutionary discoveries of the nineteenth and twentieth centuries. And that same spirit continues to inspire American scientists today.

Benjamin Franklin at his printing press

chapter 2

Colonial American Medicine

A colonial American doctor cares for
a sick patient.

In Europe, professional healers were divided into three groups: doctors, surgeons, and *apothecaries*. Doctors were professionals who had been trained in medicine at a European university. Surgeons treated broken bones, cuts, and wounds. Apothecaries mixed and sold drugs. In Europe, people went to the doctor when they were sick, to the surgeon when they were injured, and to the apothecary when they needed medicine. In the colonies, however, there were fewer healers and fewer patients. As a result, doctors did everything—they treated illnesses, set broken bones, and mixed their own drugs.

A colonial American doctor prepares an herbal remedy for a patient.

The bark of this willow tree contains a substance that can be used to cure headaches.

The Advantages of Folk Medicine

In the 1600s and 1700s, European doctors often used plants to cure diseases and relieve symptoms. They hoped that plants discovered in the Americas would provide new cures for illnesses. Colonial doctors were also very interested in the healing powers of American plants. To learn about the plants and their characteristics, the doctors paid close attention to *folk medicine*.

Many folk remedies seem absurd to us today. One suggested that the rough surface of green pine cones would remove wrinkles. Another claimed that eating kidney beans would strengthen the kidneys. Wolf fangs, strung around a child's neck, supposedly gave a child courage.

Although many folk remedies were useless, some actually worked. Native Americans, who knew the healing properties of many plants, taught colonists that willow bark can cure a headache. Today we know that willow bark contains salicylic acid—the primary ingredient in aspirin.

Often, folk medicine was more reliable than the facts medical students learned in the universities. At that time, European doctors believed that the body was made up of four elements—blood, phlegm, yellow bile, and black bile. A person became ill when one of the elements outweighed the other three. To cure a patient, doctors tried to restore the balance. For example, doctors believed that a fever was caused by an excess of blood. They responded by bleeding their patients. This method often brought down the fever, but it also weakened the patient and frequently resulted in death.

European doctors held rigidly to these beliefs. In America, however, most doctors were much more practical. They often allowed nature to take its course. Massachusetts ministers often prescribed fresh air, rest, and massage. Compared to European practices, these harmless recommendations were much better for the patients.

Cotton Mather and Inoculation

The American colonial population was often ravaged by *epidemics* of deadly diseases. Epidemics were especially dangerous in cities, where diseases spread quickly from one house to the next. In Boston, a Puritan minister named Cotton Mather was alarmed by the threat of smallpox, a horrible disease that could devastate a city's population within a year. Mather had learned of a new technique, called *inoculation,* that could prevent the disease. Reports about inoculation had appeared in British scientific papers. Moreover, Mather's black servant, Onesimus, told Mather that his African

Cotton Mather, a Puritan minister who lived in Boston, believed that inoculation was the best way to stop smallpox epidemics.

tribe had successfully used a similar technique. Other blacks confirmed Onesimus's story.

But inoculation seemed very risky and dangerous. It meant infecting a healthy person with smallpox from a sick patient. The healthy person would then become ill with the disease but suffer only a mild case. From then on, the patient would be *immune* to the disease. Smallpox would never threaten that person again. This process, however, was still unproven.

Many European and American doctors openly scoffed at this new idea. Mather, however, believed that it could work—and he soon received an opportunity to find out. In April 1721, a ship arrived in Boston from the West Indies. Its crew was infected with smallpox, and soon the disease spread into the city. In June, Mather appealed to Boston's doctors to begin inoculation. Several of them, especially those educated in Europe, refused. Many of the clergy, however, supported Mather. The controversy split the city. Pamphlets and newspapers were distributed, passionately arguing each side of the debate. In November, someone threw a bomb into Mather's house.

Colonial Inoculation

Inoculation was an uncomfortable process. First a needle was drawn through the open sore of someone suffering from smallpox. Then, the infected needle was passed through the tissue of a healthy person. This gave the person a weakened form of smallpox. Most of the time, the healthy person became sick but overcame the disease. From then on, that person was immune to smallpox.

This pamphlet describing the symptoms of and recommended treatment for smallpox was printed and distributed in 1677.

A
BRIEF RULE

To guide the Common·People of

NEW·ENGLAND

How to order themselves and theirs in the

Small Pocks, or Measels.

The small Pox (whose nature and cure the *Measels* follow) is a disease in the blood, endeavouring to recover a new form and state.
2. This nature attempts—1. By Separation of the impure from the pure, thrusting it out from the Veins to the Flesh.—2. By driving out the impure from the Flesh to the Skin.

3. The first Separation is done in the first four dayes by a Feaverish boyling (Ebullition) of the Blood, laying down the impurities in the Fleshy parts which kindly effected the Feaverish tumult is calmed.

4. The second Separation from the Flesh to the Skin, or *Superficies* is done through the rest of the time of the disease.

5. There are several Errors in ordering these sick ones in both these Operations of Nature which prove very dangerous and commonly deadly either by overmuch hastening Nature beyond its own pace, or in hindering of it from its own vigorous operation.

6. The Separation by Ebullition in the Feaverish heat is over heightened by too much Clothes, too hot a room hot *Cordials*, as *Diascordium*, *Gascons powder* and such like, for hence come *Phrensies*, dangerous excessive sweats, or the flowing of the Pocks into one overspreading fore, vulgarly called the Flox.

7. The same seperation is overmuch hindred by preposterous cooling that Feaverish boyling heat, by *blood letting, Glysters, Vomits, purges,* or *cooling medicines*. For though these many times hasten the coming forth of the Pox, yet they take away that supply which should keep them out till they are ripe, wherefore they sink into the deadly danger of the sick.

8. If a *Phrensie* happen, or through a *Plethorie* (that is fulness of blood) the Circulation of the blood be hindred, and thereupon the whole mass of blood choaked up, then either let blood, Or see that their diet, or medicines be not altogether cooling, but let them in no wise be heating, thereafter let him lye no otherwise covered in his bed then he was wont in health: His Chamber not made hot with fire if the weather be temperate, let him drink small Beer only warm'd with a Toft, let him fup up thin *water-gruel, or water potage* made only of Indian Flour and water, instead of *Oat-meal*: Let him eat *boild Apples*; But I would not advise at this time any medicine besides. If the excessive *Ebullition* (or boyling of his blood) will by degrees abate, and the Symptoms cease; If not, but the blood be so inraged that it will admit no delay, then either let blood (if Age will bear it) or else give some notably cooling medicine, or refresh him with more free Air.

9. But if the boiling of the blood be weak and dull that there is cause to fear it is not able to work a Separation as it's wont to be in such as have been let blood, or are fat, or Flegmatick, or brought low by some other sickness or labour of the (*Gonorrhea*) running of the Reins, or some other Evacuation. In such Cases, *Cordials* must drive them out, or they must dy.

10. In time of driving out the *Pocks* from the Flesh, here care must be had that the *Pustules* keep out in a right measure till they have attain'd their end without going in again, for that is deadly.

11. In this time take heed when the *Pustules* appear whilst not yet ripe, least by too much heat there arise a new *Ebullition* (or Feaverish boyling) for this troubles the driving out, or brings back the separated parts into the blood, or the Fleshy parts over heated are disabled from a right suppuration of lastly the temper of the blood and tone of the Flesh is so perverted that it cannot overcome and digest the matter driven out.

12. Yet on the other hand the breaking out must not be hindred, by exposing the sick unto the cold. The degree of heat must be such as is natural agrees with the temper of the fleshy parts: That which exceeds or falls short is dangerous: Therefore the season of the year, Age of the sick, and their manner of life here require a discreet and different Consideration, requiring the Counsel of an expert Physitian.

13. But if by any error a new *Ebullition* ariseth, the same art must be used to allay it as is before exprest.

14. If the *Pustules* go in and a flux of the belly follows (for else there is no such danger) then *Cordials* are to be used, yet moderate and not too often for fear of new *Ebullition*.

15. If much spitting (*Ptyalismus*) follow. you may hope all will go well, therefore by no means hinder it: Only with warm small Beer let their mouths be washed.

16. When the *Pustules* are dryed and fallen off, purge well, especially if it be in *Autumn*.

17. As soon as this disease therefore appears by its signs, let the sick abstain from Flesh and Wine, and open Air, let him use small Bear warmed with a Toft for his ordinary drink, and moderately when he desires it For fond use *water-gruel, water-potage,* and other things having no manifest hot quality, easy of digestion. boild Apples, and milk sometimes for change, but the coldness taken off. Let the use of his bed be according to the season of the year, and the multitude of the *Pocks,* or as found persons

are wont. In Summer let him rise according to custome, yet so as to be defended both from heat and cold in Excess, the disease will be the sooner over and less troublesome, for being kept in bed nourisheth the Feaverish heat and makes the Pocks break out with a painful inflamation.

18. In a colder season, and breaking forth of a multitude of *Pustules,* forcing the sick to keep his bed, let him be covered according to his custome in health a moderate fire in the winter being kindled in his Chamber, morning and Evening; neither need he keep his Arms alwayes in bed, or ly still in the same place, for fear least he should sweat which is very dangerous especially to youth.

20. Before the fourth day use no medicines to drive out, nor be too strict with the sick; for by how much the more gently the *Pustules* do grow, by so much the fuller and perfecter will the Separation be.

21. On the fourth day a gentle *Cordial* may help once given.

22. From that time a small draught of warm milk (not hot) a little dy'd with *Saffron* may be given morning and evening till the *Pustules* are come to their due greatness and ripeness.

23. When the *Pustules* begin to dry and crust, least the rotten vapours strike inward, which sometimes causeth sudden death; Take morning and evening some temperate *Cordial* as four or five spoonfuls of *Malago Wine* tinged with a little *Saffron*.

24. When the *Pustules* are dryd and fallen off, purge once and again, especially in the *Autumn Pocks.*

25. Beware of anointing with *Oils, Fatts, Ointments,* and such defensives, for keeping the corrupted matter in the *Pustules* from drying up, by the moisture, they fret deeper into the Flesh, and so make the more deep Scarrs.

26. The young and lively men that are brought to a plentiful sweat in this sickness, about the eighth day the sweat stops of it self, by no means afterwards to be drawn out again; the sick thereupon feels most troublesome disrest and anguish, and then makes abundance of water and so dyes.

Few young men and strong thus handled escape, except they fall into abundance of spitting or plentiful bleeding at the nose.

27. Signs discovering the Assault at first are beating pain in the head, Forehead and temples, pain in the back, great sleepiness, glistering of the eyes, shining glimmerings seem before them, itching of them also with tears flowing of themselves, itching of the Nose, short breath, dry Cough, oft sneezing, hoarseness, heat redness, and sense of pricking over the whole body, terrors in the sleep sorrow and restlesness, beating of the heart, Urine sometimes as in health, sometime filthy from great *Ebullition,* and all this or many of these with a Feaverish distemper.

28. Signs warning of the probable Event. If they break forth easily, quickly, and soon come to ripening, if the Symptomes be gentle, the Feaver mild, and after the breaking forth abates: If the voice be free, and breathing easie, especially if the Pox be red white distinct, soft few, round, sharp top'd, only without and not in the inward parts; if there be large bleeding at the nose. These signs are hopeful

29. But such signs are doubtful, when they difficulty appear, when they sink in again when they are black, blewish, green, hard, all in one, if the Feaver abate not with their breaking forth. if there be Swooning, difficulty of breathing, great thirst, quinsey, great unquietness, and if it is very dangerous, if there be ioyn'd with it some other malignant Feaver, called by some the pestilential Pox; the Spotted Feaver is oft joyned with it.

30. Deadly Signs if the Flux of the Belly happen, when they are broke forth, if the Urine be bloody or black, or the *Ordure* of that Colour; Or if pure blood be cast out by the Belly or Gumms: These Signs are for the most part deadly.

These things have I written Candid Reader, not to inform the Learned Physitian that hath much more cause to understand what pertains to this disease than I, but to give some light to those that have not such advantages, leaving the difficulty of this disease to the Physitians Art, wisdom, and Faithfulness: for the right managing of them in the whole Course of this disease tends both to the Patients safety, and the Physitians desired Success in his Administrations: For in vain is the Physitians Art Imployed, if they are not under a Regular Regiment. I am, though no Physitian, yet a well wisher to the sick. And therefore intreating the Lord to turn our hearts, and stay his hand, I am

21. 11. 167⅞.

A Friend, Reader to thy Welfare,

Thomas Thacher.

BOSTON, Printed and sold by *John Foster.* 1677

18

Despite the violence, Mather decided to inoculate several people. In 1722, after the epidemic had faded, Mather was pleased with the results. Of the 300 people he inoculated, only 6 died. The rest were protected from the terrible disease.

News of the success in Boston spread to the other colonies. In 1738, smallpox broke out in Charleston, South Carolina. The city's doctors responded quickly by inoculating large groups of people. Of the 1,000 citizens treated, only 10 died.

Despite severe criticism and opposition, Mather's experiment had proved a success. It also inspired doctors to believe that smallpox and other terrible diseases could be controlled. Later, some historians claimed that Mather was the "first significant figure in American medicine."

chapter 3

Cataloging the Life of a Continent

A North American turtle drawn by
William Bartram

European Science Comes to Colonial America

The European discovery of North America excited many scientists. Impatiently and eagerly they asked questions. What kind of animals lived there? What kind of plant life covered the countryside? Who were the native peoples, and what were their customs?

In Europe, most forests had been cleared centuries earlier. In North America, however, thick forests stretched for hundreds of miles. To the Europeans, North America seemed pure and untouched, begging for study.

In colonial times, thick forests covered most of North America. Many of these forests still stand today.

As the American colonies grew in size and population, European *natural historians* became very interested in North America. Natural historians study animal and plant life. At the time the American colonies were being settled, natural historians in Europe were beginning to catalog Earth's wildlife in a new way. A Swedish scientist named Carolus Linnaeus had recently proposed grouping living things together according to similarities in physical appearance and behavior.

Carolus Linnaeus developed the most commonly used system for identifying and classifying living things.

Linnaeus gave each *organism* a name that consisted of two Latin words. The first word indicated the organism's *genus;* the second word identified the organism's *species.* This classification system, called *taxonomy,* is still used today. With the Linnaean system, European scientists planned to catalog all life throughout the world.

At first, most samples of North American wildlife were collected by visiting Europeans. After returning to Europe, they wrote books describing their explorations and discoveries. These books became very popular and were widely read. But toward the end of the 1600s, Europeans found a way to avoid the long, costly, and dangerous journey to North America. They asked the American colonists to collect samples for them.

Colonial American science began with the simple act of exploration. Acting more like collectors than creators of new theories, the first American scientists went to work. They ventured into the dense forests for weeks or months at a time, collecting samples of plant and animal life and sending them to scientists in Europe.

Peter Collinson Helps American Scientists

Many American scientists were supported by members of the Royal Society of London. With the Society's encouragement and money, colonial Americans spent weeks in the North American wilderness. They collected leaves, flowers, and seeds and sent them to England and other countries in Europe. In 1735, a London Quaker merchant named Peter Collinson began to organize American efforts in natural history.

Collinson was passionately interested in flowers and trees—especially rare and unusual species. He requested samples of plants and animals from his American business friends and was soon receiving hundreds of specimens. Collinson loved to spend time in his London warehouse, writing letters and studying the latest samples

Peter Collinson

of wildlife sent from North America. Natural historians throughout Europe wrote to Collinson, asking for seeds and plants for their gardens.

Soon, Collinson became an important figure in American science. As a member of the Royal Society, Collinson used his position to support American efforts in natural history. He made sure that American collectors received credit for their work. Through Collinson's attention, an American scientist named John Bartram became known around the world.

John Bartram: Father of American Botany

John Bartram, who was born in 1699, grew up on the rich Pennsylvania farmland outside Philadelphia. Supposedly, Bartram first became interested in plants when his plow overturned a daisy. The structure of the plant's leaves and delicate petals fascinated him. Inspired, Bartram traveled to Philadelphia, where he read several books on *botany,* including one that taught him the Linnaean system of classification.

In 1728, Bartram purchased a plot of land at Kingsessing, which is a few miles outside Philadelphia. He laid out a garden and began growing plants. In one experiment, he sprinkled the pollen seeds of one plant

John Bartram spent many years searching the American countryside for new types of plants and animals.

24

George Washington (left) visited John Bartram's garden in 1774.

onto another plant's flower. The result was a brand-new kind of plant. Today, this process—called *hybridization*—is widely used by scientists.

Bartram began making expeditions into the deep wilderness to find new plants. He frequently went in autumn, when the seeds were easy to find and flower bulbs were easy to dig up. After returning home, Bartram planted the seeds and bulbs in his own garden.

Bartram's samples drew Peter Collinson's attention, and the two began exchanging long letters filled with observations on plants. Soon, Bartram's samples were distributed in Europe. Collinson sold Bartram's seeds to

William Bartram drew many of the plants and animals that he and his father discovered as they explored the North American wilderness. These sketches show a final painting of an evening primrose (left) and rough sketches of a black vulture (top).

English landowners, who planted them in their gardens. Collinson faithfully sent the money from these sales to Bartram.

In 1765, Bartram received a pension from the King of England as the official botanist of the American colonies. Free to spend several months exploring, Bartram traveled as far north as the Great Lakes and as far south as the Spanish territory of Florida. Everywhere he went, Bartram discovered new species of wildlife. Frequently, he brought his son along to make detailed drawings of their findings. Bartram carefully packed his samples—plants, insects, rocks, and minerals—in boxes and sent them to England.

In honor of his work, Bartram was elected to the Royal Academy of Sciences in Stockholm, Sweden, and given a medal by the Edinburgh Society of Arts and Sciences. Linnaeus called Bartram the "greatest natural botanist in the world." Today, Bartram is called the "father of American botany." He was one of the first American scientists to gain fame in Europe, and his work inspired other Americans to follow in his footsteps. One of those people was Thomas Jefferson.

Thomas Jefferson

Thomas Jefferson was born in 1743, and raised in central Virginia. As a young boy, he enjoyed roaming through the mountains and forests around his home. A multitalented genius, Jefferson achieved brilliance in several different fields. Today, we also remember Jefferson as the author of the Declaration of Independence.

As a young man, Jefferson developed a passionate interest in science. At his home, Monticello, in Virginia, he pursued new techniques in farming and raising animals. Like other philosophers of his time, Jefferson believed

Monticello, the home built by Thomas Jefferson

that the study of science would greatly benefit humanity. He also believed that science should be practical. "Science never appears so beautiful," he once wrote, "as when applied to the uses of human life."

In 1780, Jefferson received a request from a French statesman. He wanted Jefferson to answer several questions about the people, climate, plants and animals, and landscape of Virginia. Jefferson answered these questions in the form of a book called *Notes on the State of Virginia*. It was printed in France in 1781.

Jefferson's book discussed such topics as religion, slavery, Native Americans, geology, wildlife, farming, and education. In clear and precise language, Jefferson presented a vivid portrait of his beloved state. He noted the size of the animals and the most common types of trees. He discussed the various landscapes, such as the rolling mountains in the west and the tidewater regions along Chesapeake Bay. Jefferson also rejected widely accepted European theories that North America was a crippled continent of stunted trees, small animals, and simple people.

Despite the popularity of Jefferson's *Notes,* the leading French natural historian, Georges du Buffon, continued to describe North America as inferior. Stung by Buffon's remarks, Jefferson decided to prove the Frenchman wrong. From Paris, he sent letters to friends in the United States, requesting that they send him "the skin, the skeleton, and the horns" of several large North American animals. Jefferson confidently predicted that one North American moose would quickly prove Buffon wrong.

The animals arrived, but Jefferson was disappointed. He had anticipated larger and more impressive samples. Again he wrote to the United States, requesting larger specimens. Jefferson's friends shipped another moose to France. This time, Jefferson was pleased, and he displayed the 7-foot (2.1-m)-tall animal in the lobby of his hotel. Buffon inspected the specimen, but remained unconvinced.

Georges du Buffon, a prominent French natural historian, lived from 1707 to 1788.

Jefferson Studies Ancient Bones

As he looked for evidence that North America was not inferior to Europe, Jefferson made several discoveries. While still in France, he sponsored a North American expedition to locate fossilized bones of extinct animals. Jefferson was convinced that woolly mammoths, huge elephant-like animals, had once lived in North America. To his great delight, mammoth bones were discovered and sent to France. Jefferson even claimed that the woolly mammoth still existed in unexplored regions of North America.

He listened with great interest to Indian and pioneer stories about "terrible roarings" and "eyes like two balls of fire."

Jefferson continued to be fascinated by ancient bones after his return to the United States. In 1796, he received a collection of unusual bones that had been discovered in western Virginia. He called the animal *Megalonyx,* which is a Latin word meaning "giant claw." Jefferson was confident that this animal, a giant ground sloth, had not yet been identified by science.

An artist's representation of a giant ground sloth

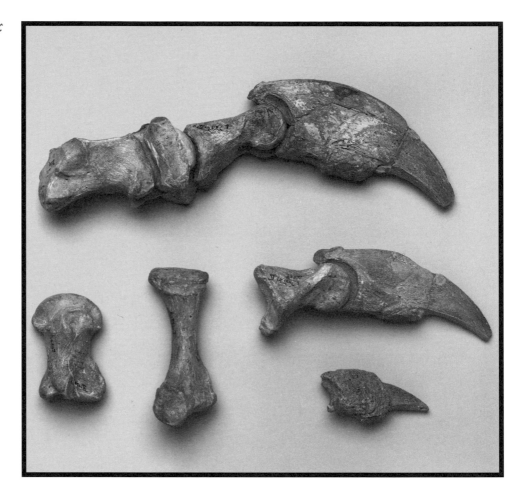

Bones of *Megalonyx jeffersonii;* the extinct giant ground sloth named after Thomas Jefferson.

In 1797, Jefferson brought the bones with him to Philadelphia, where he was being sworn in as vice president of the United States. He planned to announce his discovery of the *Megalonyx* to the American Philosophical Society. Before he could, though, Jefferson read a London magazine. In its pages, he discovered an illustration of an animal that appeared similar to his *Megalonyx.* The author of the article had identified the animal from bones discovered in South America almost 10 years earlier. That scientist called the animal *Megatherium.*

Jefferson changed some details of his paper and read it to the American Philosophical Society. Years later, Jefferson was honored for the discovery of

Thomas Jefferson had many different interests. He enjoyed studying living plants and animals as well as fossils of extinct creatures. In 1801, he became the third president of the United States.

Megalonyx. A French scientist used the Linnaean system to name Jefferson's skeleton *Megalonyx jeffersonii.* After Jefferson's death, he was honored in France for his tremendous contributions to their collection of ancient fossils.

Jefferson remained passionately interested in natural history when he became president of the United States in 1801. He was convinced that the western half of North America contained new species of animal life waiting to be discovered. In 1803, Jefferson made a historic purchase of land from Napoleon I, who ruled France. The Louisiana Purchase doubled the size of

Wild blue flax, which can be found near the headwaters of the Missouri River, were first identified by Lewis and Clark.

the United States. In 1804, Jefferson launched one of the most famous exploratory journeys of all time—the Lewis and Clark Expedition of the northwestern United States.

Natural history was the first true science practiced in America. It promoted scientific ties between Europe and North America. The first Americans to win general praise in Europe studied natural science.

When natural scientists ventured into the wilderness, they were often accompanied by traders and trappers who depended on astronomy and math to map the continent and navigate its mighty rivers. As the colonial American population grew and settlers spread westward, they too needed maps. As a result, more and more colonists began to look up at the star-filled sky.

Grouse are about short and eye. Cock Cock which on the and hood Mountains to the Mountain the Columbia the Great falls they go in Large or singularly hide hide remarkably close when pursued. short flights &c.

the feathers about its head pointed and stiff some hairs the base of the beak. feathers fine and stiff about the ears, This is a faint likeness of the of the plains or Heath the first of those fowls we met with was Missouri below in the neighbour= of the Rocky and from which paps between and Rapids Gorges and make

The large Black & White Pheasant is peculiar to that portion of the Rocky Mountains watered by the Columbia River. at least we did not see them until we reached the waters of that river, nor since we have left those mountains. they are about the size of a well grown hen. the contour of the bird is much that of the red & brown Pheasant common to our country. the tail is proportionably as long and is

A page from the journal William Clark kept during his expedition of the northwestern United States

chapter 4
Astronomy: The Search for Respect

The colonists relied on their knowledge
of the stars to navigate ships and
guide them across the North American
wilderness.

The study of astronomy was very important in colonial America. In port cities, navigators used the stars to guide their ships. As the colonists expanded westward, they required precise calculations to determine boundaries and property lines. The English astronomers Charles Mason and Jeremiah Dixon used their science skills to draw the boundary between the colonies of Pennsylvania and Maryland. Today, this border is called the Mason-Dixon line.

Some colonial Americans became well known in Europe by studying the night sky. In 1680, Thomas Brattle observed a *comet,* and carefully recorded its position as it moved across the night sky. Later, English scientist Isaac Newton used Brattle's precise observations in his landmark scientific work, *Principia. Principia* discussed the mathematical laws that rule the universe. It was hailed throughout Europe as one of the greatest works of science ever written.

While many colonial Americans made practical use of astronomy, very few made new

Charles Mason and Jeremiah Dixon lay the boundary line between the colonies of Pennsylvania and Maryland in the 1760s.

discoveries. By the 1760s, however, the colonies had grown larger and wealthier. Buying expensive telescopes and constructing elaborate observatories were no longer out of the question. In that decade, David Rittenhouse and other colonial American scientists made some significant contributions to the science of astronomy.

Rittenhouse and the Orrery

Born in 1732, David Rittenhouse grew up in Pennsylvania. From an early age, he demonstrated an astonishing ability with numbers. By the time he was 17 years old, he had begun building clocks, which he sold to local farmers and townspeople. Although he had no formal education, Rittenhouse mastered the basic rules of math.

David Rittenhouse made tremendous contributions to colonial American astronomy.

Rittenhouse's brilliance impressed a man named Thomas Barton. He encouraged Rittenhouse by giving him books about mathematics and philosophy. He also urged Rittenhouse to move to Philadelphia. In this bustling city, Rittenhouse could find support and meet other intellectuals while he studied science. But Rittenhouse rejected Barton's advice. He continued to build clocks and pursue his own experiments.

Despite his decision to remain outside Philadelphia, Rittenhouse's talent was soon noticed anyway. In 1763, he was hired by the state of Pennsylvania to *survey* state boundaries. Rittenhouse quickly became respected for the precision and accuracy of his measurements.

In 1766, Rittenhouse began planning to build a mechanical model of the solar system, called an *orrery*. An orrery was used as an aid during lectures. By depicting the paths of the planets, teachers could demonstrate how the solar system functions. Several orreries had already been constructed in Europe. Rittenhouse, however, confidently predicted that his orrery would be the most accurate in the world. Rittenhouse's friends in Philadelphia learned of his project and were impressed. In 1767, they

This orrery shows the positions and orbital paths of the planets known at the time it was built.

awarded him an honorary degree from the College of Philadelphia. Encouraged by the honor, Rittenhouse began to build his model.

Using his skill and experience as a clockmaker, Rittenhouse constructed each known planet out of balls of brass and ivory. He carefully plotted the planets' orbit and their speed as they revolve around the sun. When the orrery was finished, it amazed observers. By winding a simple crank, viewers watched the solar system move like a precise clock. Rittenhouse's calculations were extremely accurate. The orrery could predict and show each planet's position 5,000 years into the past and 5,000 years into the future.

Both the College of Philadelphia and the College of New Jersey (now called Princeton University) wanted to purchase Rittenhouse's orrery. The two schools competed for the honor of owning Rittenhouse's model. Eventually, the College of Philadelphia won. It received the first orrery, and Rittenhouse built a second model for the College of New Jersey.

Newspapers praised Rittenhouse as a "singular genius," and Thomas Jefferson would later proclaim that Rittenhouse was "second to no astronomer living." To Americans, the orreries proved that the serious study of science could take place in the colonies. Rittenhouse's success encouraged interest in astronomy throughout colonial America. This interest became focused on an approaching astronomical event of great importance—the *transit of Venus.*

The Transit of Venus

In 1769, colonial Americans anticipated a rare and important astronomical event. The planet Venus was about to pass between Earth and the sun. This occurrence was called the transit of Venus, and it offered a tremendous opportunity. By observing the transit and measuring the exact amount of time it took, scientists could calculate the distance from the sun to Earth. To accurately record the transit, several calculations had to be made at the same time over vast distances.

Colonial American scientists planned to send expeditions to different parts of the continent to observe the event. If American scientists could record the transit accurately, they would win honor and respect in Europe.

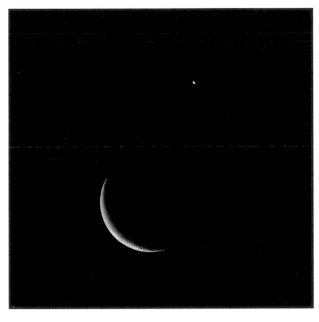

Here, the planet Venus can be seen above the crescent moon.

Throughout the colonies, scientists made preparations. In large cities, such as Boston and Philadelphia, the observation would be recorded by telescopes. In the countryside, most people planned to calculate the transit with watches and measuring tools.

Colonial newspapers reported information on the transit and advised how best to record it. As the day drew near, people prepared smoked glass to observe the sun without harming their eyes. In large cities, citizens gathered around the scientists to watch them work.

The day of the transit dawned bright and clear. As Venus passed across the face of the sun, colonial Americans from Massachusetts to Georgia took measurements. In Philadelphia, America's greatest astronomer, David Rittenhouse, watched carefully through his telescope. To observe the transit perfectly, he lay on the floor with his head supported by assistants. He had remained in this position for several minutes before the transit suddenly began. In a rush of emotion, Rittenhouse fainted. Although he quickly recovered consciousness and recorded the time, he could not determine the precise length of the transit.

Throughout the colonies, people recorded their calculations and sent them to local newspapers. But there were several problems. Many of the colonists' observations had been made with inaccurate clocks and instruments. In Philadelphia, Rittenhouse gathered the calculations and came up with an estimate of 93 million miles (149,664,900 km). This result is actually extremely close to the actual distance—92,956,000 miles (149,594,090 km).

All across Europe, news of the American observations was greeted with surprise and praise. The colonists had displayed a spirit of cooperation in the pursuit of science. American scientist William Smith exclaimed that the observation had "done a credit to our country!"

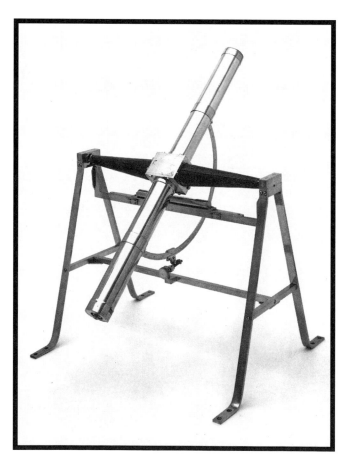

David Rittenhouse built this telescope and viewed the transit of Venus through it in 1769.

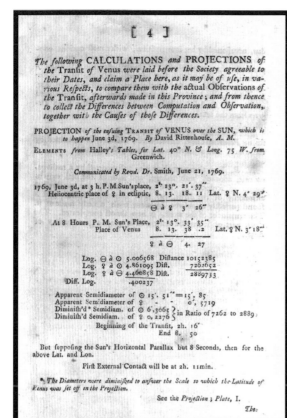

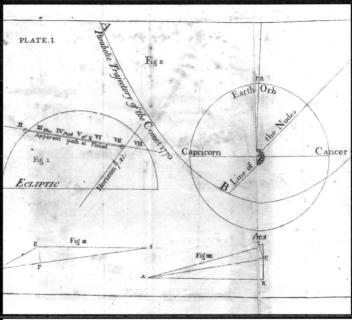

After the transit of Venus, David Rittenhouse estimated the distance between the sun and Earth. His results were published in the *Transactions of the American Philosophical Society*.

Despite this success, Rittenhouse and colonial American scientists made few other revolutionary contributions to the study of astronomy. Astronomy required knowledge and resources the colonies still did not have. However, colonial Americans contributed a great deal to newer sciences. One extremely clever man from Philadelphia would define a new science, earning him and the American colonies respect around the globe. That man—Benjamin Franklin—became the most famous scientist to emerge from colonial America.

chapter 5

Electricity: The New Science

Benjamin Franklin is best remembered
for his electricity experiments.

It's a dry winter day. You shuffle across a carpet and then reach out and touch a door knob. Zap! You feel a small shock of electricity. Today, we know quite a bit about electricity, but in the 1740s, it fascinated and baffled Europeans. They watched in amazement as a traveling lecturer created a small spark and pop by simply rubbing a glass rod against his clothing and then touching it.

While visiting Boston in 1743, Benjamin Franklin watched a Scottish scientist named Dr. Archibald Spencer perform all sorts of spectacular electrical experiments. Curious at this display of "shocks" and "magic," Franklin bought Spencer's equipment and brought it home to Philadelphia.

In 1746, Franklin ordered more complex equipment from England. Franklin's interest centered on a device called a Leyden jar. A Leyden jar is a small jar filled with water. The jar is sealed with a cork that has a chain running through it. One end of the chain hangs in the water. The other end of the chain is attached to a rod above the jar. When the water in the jar is charged with electricity, it can produce a giant shock. Reportedly, one shock from a Leyden jar made 180 French guardsmen jump into the air at the same time.

Franklin Experiments with the Leyden Jar

Franklin wondered how the Leyden jar worked. Normally, colonial American scientists were at a serious disadvantage. Because there were few centers of learning in the colonies, news of important theories and discov-

Benjamin Franklin built this battery using thirty-five Leyden jars.

eries made in Europe often took months to reach scientists in colonial America. But for Benjamin Franklin, working in the colonies proved to be an advantage. Away from European intellectuals and scientists, Franklin asked questions that no one had ever dreamed about before.

His first question was simple. Where was the electricity? Was it in the water, the glass, or the metal? Franklin used common sense to design the experiments that could answer his question. He charged the jar with electricity and removed the cork and chain. Carefully, he placed his finger near the water. A small spark jumped. Franklin now knew that the electricity was not in the chain or the cork. That left two possibilities—the water or the glass jar holding the water.

Franklin set up another experiment. He charged the jar again, but placed uncharged water in it. The glass sparked. Franklin now knew that the electrical spark was in the glass.

One question still challenged Franklin. Was the glass itself causing the spark, or was it the shape of the glass? To test this, Franklin charged a flat piece of glass from a windowpane. On both sides of the glass, he placed thin sheets of lead. Each time he stripped off a sheet of lead, he looked for electrical sparks. None came. But when the glass was finally uncovered, sparks flew. Franklin had his answer. He wrote: "The whole force and power of giving a shock is in the glass itself."

Franklin's observation was critically important. Until then, European scientists had believed that there were different kinds of electricity, each existing in separate materials. Franklin united these theories by recognizing electricity as a single force. To describe the effects of electricity, Franklin used terms that are still familiar today— resistance, conductor, battery, electric shock, and electrician. He also described positive and negative charge.

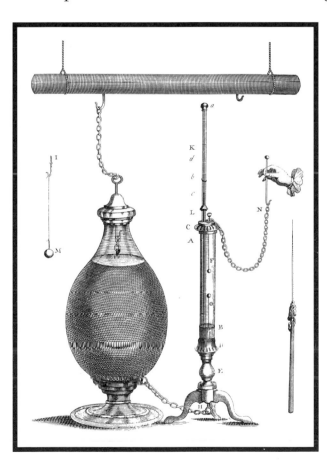

This drawing of a Leyden jar appeared in a pamphlet in which Franklin described his experiments.

Franklin Publishes His Results

In 1751, Franklin published his experiments in a simple pamphlet called *Experiments and Observations on Electricity.* The pamphlet was an instant success. It drew a great deal of attention in the colonies and in Europe. One Englishman noted with astonishment that Franklin had removed "all mystery . . . from the subject. . . . His details [are] elegant as well as simple."

Because the news took 3 months to travel by ship, Franklin had no idea how Europeans had reacted to his ideas. Nevertheless, he continued to perform experiments with electricity. One of these would make him famous.

In his pamphlet, Franklin had proposed that the lightning in clouds was actually electricity. This may seem obvious to us today, but at that time, lightning was a mysterious and terrifying force. Without warning, lightning struck buildings, caused fires, and occasionally hit and killed animals and people. Most people believed that lightning was a sign of God's displeasure. Many priests rang church bells during thunderstorms in the frantic hope of warding off destruction.

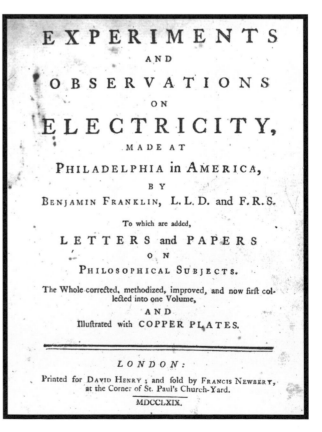

The title page from Franklin's famous pamphlet

Franklin became famous for explaining the cause of lightning.

Franklin, however, suspected that clouds became electrified, just like the Leyden jar. In his pamphlet, Franklin proposed an experiment that could prove his theory. He suggested mounting a *sentry box* on a high tower. Inside, a person would sit sheltered from the storm. From the box, a rod would extend upward 20 to 30 feet (6 to 9 m). If a low thundercloud passed over, the rod should "draw sparks, draw fire . . . from [the] cloud." This would prove that lightning from clouds, like the spark from the charged Leyden jar, was electricity.

To perform his experiment, Franklin eagerly awaited the completion of the steeple in Christ Church, Philadelphia. In Paris, however, a young French scientist did not need to wait. Francis D'Abilard read Franklin's pamphlet and decided to carry out the experiment himself. On May 10, 1752, D'Abilard sat in a sentry box with a metal rod pointed toward the sky. A thunderstorm roared overhead. Suddenly, the rod in front of D'Abilard glowed blue as a lightning charge struck it. Franklin's experiment was a success!

D'Abilard performing Benjamin Franklin's experiment

The experiment was repeated for the king of France and again for the king of England. For years, people had attempted to show that lightning and electricity were actually the same. With his simple experiment, Franklin had proved it. Suddenly, Mr. Benjamin Franklin of Philadelphia was world famous.

Franklin's Kite Experiment

Franklin, however, was still unaware of his own success. Impatient at the slow work at Christ Church, he decided to get results in a different way.

Franklin attached a piece of wire to the head of a small kite. At the other end of the string, he tied a small key with a piece of silk. At the next sign of a storm, he and his son William rushed to an open field outside Philadelphia. Sitting in a shepherd's hut, Franklin watched as William ran back and forth three times, trying to get the kite to fly. Finally, as the dark clouds approached, the kite hovered in the air. Franklin and William waited. When a very low cloud passed over the kite, the threads of the string suddenly stood on end.

Benjamin Franklin and his son, William, testing his idea that lightning is a form of electricity.

Had the experiment worked? Franklin moved his finger toward the key. Zap! To Franklin and William's delight, a spark flew. The experiment had worked.

Franklin developed a practical use for his discovery. By running a metal wire down the side of a building to the ground, structures could avoid the damage caused by a lightning strike. Franklin had invented the *lightning rod*. He described the invention in his almanac and urged all citizens to put lightning rods on their houses.

People all over the world were impressed and astonished by Franklin's discoveries. John Adams wrote that the lightning rod "disarmed the clouds of heaven." Franklin received honorary degrees from Harvard and Yale universities in 1753. A year later, the Royal Society in London awarded him the Copley Gold Medal.

In 1754, Benjamin Franklin received the Copley Medal from the Royal Society of London.

Franklin's experiment proved that widely accepted superstitions about lightning and its mysterious, terrifying power were wrong. It also proved that Sir Francis Bacon had been right. Bacon had believed that the study of science would make people's lives better. Some people had criticized Bacon, insisting that science did nothing more than provide answers to useless questions. Franklin's experiment helped change this attitude. Using what he learned by studying electricity, Franklin had invented the lightning rod—a device that helped everyone.

Franklin's success also proved to Europe and to the world that the American colonies could produce great scientists on their own. One European wrote to Franklin: "Go on making experiments on your own . . . and thereby pursue a path entirely different from the Europeans." Ben Franklin's discoveries helped the American colonies earn the respect of the Europeans.

chapter 6

American Science Comes of Age

American colonists cutting trees in
a New England forest

Science in colonial America was shaped by the demands of early colonial life. Faced with the exhausting task of clearing the wilderness and building towns, colonial Americans needed practical science. Difficult experiments and elaborate theories were useless. Americans demanded that their science be simple and useful.

Colonial American science was also democratic. The transit of Venus was observed and measured by hundreds of colonists. Their observations made it possible to calculate the distance between Earth and the sun with great precision. Benjamin Franklin's experiments and revolutionary discoveries did not require elaborate laboratories or expensive equipment. In fact, he made one of the most important discoveries of the eighteenth century with materials found in most colonial American homes—a key, a simple kite, and a ball of string.

Another factor influencing colonial science was America's distance from Europe. Colonial American scientists often took risks and asked questions that did not occur to European scientists. Benjamin Franklin's separation from European centers of learning allowed him to approach the science of electricity in a whole new way.

American science in the 1800s kept many of the characteristics developed in the 1700s. It remained very practical. Americans invented new machines and figured out ways to solve common problems. Throughout the world, Americans became known for their "can-do" spirit and their ability to overcome obstacles.

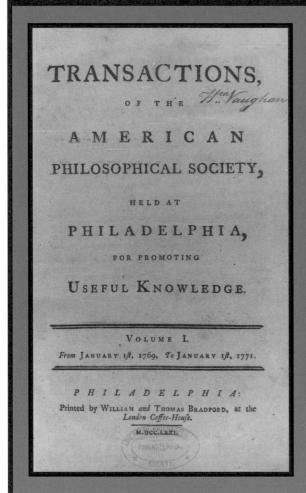

In 1769, American colonists took a critically important step for the study of science—they formed the American Philosophical Society in Philadelphia. Like the scientific societies in Europe, the American Philosophical Society was dedicated to the advancement of knowledge. It is the oldest scientific society in the United States. Among its presidents were John Bartram and Thomas Jefferson. Today, the American Philosophical Society still promotes the study of science and knowledge throughout the world.

The American Philosophical Society of America published a wide variety of important scientific findings.

The spirit of colonial American science is still present in American science today. In the twentieth century, American science has produced a staggering number of discoveries and inventions. From artificial hearts to supercomputers to the Space Shuttle, Americans have led the world in the quest to learn about ourselves, our world, and our universe.

The American Space Shuttle *Discovery* lifting off from the Kennedy Space Center in Florida.

GLOSSARY

apothecary—a person who prepares and sells drugs.

astronomy—the study of objects outside Earth's atmosphere.

botany—the study of plants.

colonist—a person who lives in a new territory that is governed by an established country. The American colonies were ruled by Britain.

comet—a ball of ice and rock that orbits around the sun.

democratic—involving everyone, not just a small group.

epidemic—an outbreak of infectious disease that spreads quickly through a population.

folk medicine—a tradition of medicine practiced by healers who are not trained as doctors.

genus—a group of living things that has similar characteristics and behaviors. A genus can be subdivided into species.

hybridization—a process in which two organisms are bred to create a new species.

immune—to be successfully resistant to a disease.

inoculation—introducing a disease into a person's body so that he or she will become immune to it.

lightning rod—a metal rod or wire that allows lightning to travel to the ground without damaging a building.

natural historian—a scientist who studies animals, plants, and geology.

natural philosopher—a term once used to describe anyone who studied science, particularly science relating to the natural world.

organism—a living thing.

orrery—a mechanical model of the solar system.

philosopher—a person who seeks wisdom by studying or thinking about the world and the relationship of humans to other creatures.

sentry box—a small shelter for a guard (sentry).

species—a group of creatures within a genus that share certain characteristics and behaviors. The members of a species can mate and produce healthy young.

survey—to determine the area of a plot of land using mathematical calculations.

taxonomy—the study of how living things are related to one another.

transit of Venus—the passage of the planet Venus between Earth and the sun.

RESOURCES

Books

Alderman, Clifford L. *Story of the Thirteen Colonies.* New York: Random Books for Young Readers, 1966.

Brown, Gene. *Discovery and Settlement: Europe Meets the New World.* New York: Twenty-first Century Books, 1993.

Kallen, Stuart. *Life in the Thirteen Colonies.* Minneapolis: Abdo and Daughters, 1990.

Kalman, Bobbie. *Colonial Life.* New York: Crabtree Publishing Company, 1992.

Osbourne, Mary P. *The Many Lives of Benjamin Franklin.* New York: Dial Books for Young Readers, 1990.

Smith, Carter. *Arts and Sciences: A Sourcebook on Colonial America.* Brookfield, CT: Millbrook Press, 1991.

Internet Sites

The World of Benjamin Franklin presents several topics on Benjamin Franklin and a link to the world-famous Franklin Institute. This site can be reached at: **http://sln.fi.edu/franklin/**

Interpreting Thomas Jefferson is a website featuring Clay Jenkinson, who has performed as Thomas Jefferson to great praise. Its address is: **http://www.th-jefferson.org/**

Thomas Jefferson Online is the site of the PBS documentary on Thomas Jefferson by Ken Burns. Its address is: **http://www.pbs.org/jefferson/**

INDEX

ABOUT THE AUTHOR

Brendan January was born and raised in Pleasantville, New York. He attended Haverford College, where he received a B.A. in history and English. He has written more than a dozen children's books about American history. This is his second book for Franklin Watts.